Da'thy's
Mississippi Soul Food

Dorothy Woods

Da'thy's Mississippi Soul Food
Copyright © 2022 by Dorothy Woods

Library of Congress Control Number: 2022909669
ISBN-13: Paperback: 978-1-64749-771-2
          ePub: 978-1-64749-772-9

All rights reserved. No part of this publication may be reproduced, distributed, or transmitted in any form or by any means, including photocopying, recording, or other electronic or mechanical methods, without the prior written permission of the publisher or author, except in the case of brief quotations embodied in critical reviews and certain other noncommercial uses permitted by copyright law.

Although every precaution has been taken to verify the accuracy of the information contained herein, the author and publisher assume no responsibility for any errors or omissions. No liability is assumed for damages that may result from the use of information contained within.

Printed in the United States of America

GoToPublish LLC
1-888-337-1724
www.gotopublish.com
info@gotopublish.com

CONTENTS

Introduction vii
Celebrating Achievements ix
Appetizer 1
    Clam Fritters 2
    Sweet and Sour Chicken Wings 3
Breakfast 5
    Beef Liver and Onions 6
    Fairy Mississippi Rolls 7
    Fried Potatoes 8
    Jamiya's Fast N Easy Biscuits 9
    Scrambled Eggs with Ham 10
Dinner 11
    Baked Fish 12
    Barbecue Spareribs 13
    Big Leroy's Skillet Beef & Macaroni 14
    Boiled Pig Feet 15
    Braised Duck with Beer 16
    Breaded Veal Cutlet 17
    Buttered Beans with Chopped Ham 18
    Chicken Tetrazzini 19
    Collard Greens and Ham Hocks or Smoked Turkey Tail 20
    Collard Greens with Neck Bones 21
    Corn Oysters 22

Cornish Hen with Wild Rice 23
Cumberland Sauce 24
Da'thy's Lobster Newburg 25
Da'thy's Mississippi Baked Turkey with Oyster Stuffing 26
Da'thy's Mississippi Curry Chicken 27
Easy To Make Meat Loaf 28
Gumbo 29
Honey Baked Ham 30
Lemon Chicken 31
Meatballs N Gravy 32
Mississippi Fried Steak and Gravy 33
Mississippi Hearty Beef Stew 34
Mississippi Smothered Rabbit with Gravy 35
Mississippi Smothered Steak 36
Mixed Greens 37
Oven Fried Chicken 38
Pineapple Duck 39
Pinto Beans and Ham Hocks 40
Pork Chitterlings 41
Pork Neck Bones and Black Eyes Peas 42
Roast Hen with Stuffing 43
Sweet and Sour Meatballs 44
Turkey Parts with Rice 45
Veal with Sauce 46

Dessert 47
Apple Pie 48
Banana Nut Bread 49
Chocolate Pound Cake 50
Cottage Cheese Jell-O Salad 51
Da'thy's Can't Get Enough Peach Cobbler 52
Da'thy's Can't Stop Eat'em Candie Yams 53
Da'thy's Mississippi Pound Cake 54

   Da'thy's Mouth Watering Sweet Potato Pie 55
   German Sweet Chocolate Cake 56
   Ginger Cookies 57
   Hoe Cakes 58
   Jell-O Lemon Pudding Cake 59
   Kentucky Bourbon Sweet Potatoes 60
   Lime Pie 61
   Mississippi Banana Pudding 62
   Mississippi Pecan Pie 63
   Molasses Brown Bread 64
   Peanut Butter Bon Bars 65
   Pie Crust 66
   Pumpkin Pie 67
   Sautéed Bananas 68

Lunch... **69**
   Buttermilk Hush Puppies 70
   Chicken Casserole 71
   Chicken Gizzards with Rice 72
   Chicken with Biscuit Crisps 73
   Chili 74
   Chili Tacos 75
   Pineapple Chicken 76
   Da'thy's Quick Chicken and Dumplings 77
   Da'thy's Mississippi Fried Chicken 78
   Da'thy's Sock-It-To-Me Baked Macaroni and Cheese 79
   Da'thy's Fast Chili 80
   Da'thy's Quick Meatloaf 81
   Fried Cat Fish Nuggets 82
   Fried Chicken Gizzards 83
   Fried Fish 84
   Jessie Palmer's Bake Burgers 85
   Sausage Rice Casserole 86

    Summer Squash Casserole 87
Side **89**
    Barbeque Sauce 90
    Boston Baked Beans 91
    Burnt Sugar Syrup Topping 92
    Cabbage 93
    Chinese Stir-fry Chicken 94
    Easy Cheesy Sauce 95
    Hog Head Cheese 96
    Homemade Mashed Potatoes 97
    Mississippi Fried Corn 98
    Oyster Stuffing 99
    Pineapple Sauce 100
    Spanish Rice 101
    Zucchini Bread 102
    Zucchini with Fresh Herbs 103
Supper **105**
    Cornbread 106
    Da'thy's 7-Bone Roast 107
    Da'thy's Meat Sauce 108
Salad **109**
    Food Potato Salad 110
Afterword **111**
Index **113**
Order Form **117**

INTRODUCTION

Congratulations; by choosing this cookbook, you are beginning a series of actions that goes beyond the preparation of food. You are renewing an important heritage that is central to the essence of the Negro life.

Due to personal circumstance; I was separated from my family for several years. Upon my reconciliation, with my family, one of my daughters, Jasmine, said to me "Mommy, I missed your cooking so much! I need some 'SOUL FOOD." She brought tears to my eyes. So I made her, her favorite meal: Fried Chicken, Smother Cabbage, Candied Yams, Mac and Cheese, and Cornbread. She was so happy. She said; "I've been all over looking for some good soul food; and I can't find none like yours, mommy."

So my family talked to me about leaving a legacy for my grandchildren. We pray that this Cookbook will be a joy to you when sharing good soul food among loved ones and good friends by making each meal together a celebration.

CELEBRATING ACHIEVEMENTS

In our family, my grandson Jacoby get lots of awards: He is 7 years old. So I decided to go to his house, and cook whatever he wants; whenever he accomplishes a goal. I set aside some time and go to his house and cook. He loves my special meat sauce with spaghetti; so that's his celebratory dish. Recently, he received an achievement award, so I went to cook for him. He started teasing his brothers and sisters, "You are enjoying this good meal because of me!"

My grandsons' dish:

My grandsons' favorite dish is macaroni and cheese: They say, "My favorite dish is macaroni and cheese, as prepared by my Grandma," says my grandsons, Ray Ray, Elishujah, Raishaun, Raiquan, and Nejan.

We only have macaroni and cheese on special occasions because I use at least three cheeses: its thick, golden mixture that is moist, but firm. For all holidays, it's a must.

APPETIZER

Clam Fritters

2 egg yolks, beaten
1/2 cup milk
1/2 teaspoon instant minced onion
2 cans minced clams, drained
1 cup bread crumbs, dried
1 tablespoon snipped fresh parsley
1 teaspoon salt
1/2 teaspoon pepper
1/4 teaspoon dried thyme, crushed
2 egg whites, stiffly beaten
1 Crisco oil

Instructions:
Combine egg yolks, milk, and onion in large bowl. Let stand 5 minutes. Stir in clams, bread crumbs, parsley, salt, pepper and thyme. Fold in egg whites. Heat 1/4 inch Crisco oil to 365F in deep skillet. Drop batter by tablespoonfuls, a few at a time, into oil. Fry until golden brown. Turn once. Garnish with orange slices, if desired.

Serves 4.

Sweet and Sour Chicken Wings

5 pounds chicken wings or drumettes
2 cups corn-starch
2 teaspoons garlic salt
1 teaspoon fresh ground black pepper
4 egg(s), beaten
1/2 cup vegetable oil
3 teaspoons salt
1 cup cider vinegar
2 tablespoons soy sauce
1 cup sugar
6 tablespoons ketchup
1/2 cup chicken stack

Instructions:
Preheat oven to 350 degrees. Cut each chicken wing into 3 sections. Reserve the wing tips to make stock. Dip the other chicken pieces in beaten eggs. Roll each piece in corn-starch and fry golden brown. Transfer chicken to baking dish. Mix garlic salt, pepper, and salt; then sprinkle evenly over chicken.

Sauce:
Combine chicken stock, cider vinegar, soy sauce, sugar, ketchup, and 2 tsp of salt; Pour over chicken. Bake in oven 30 minutes.

BREAKFAST

Beef Liver and Onions

4 slices beef liver
1 teaspoon salt
1 tablespoon seasoning salt
1/2 cup flour
2 medium onions
1 teaspoon black pepper
1 teaspoon accent
1/3 cup vegetable oil

Instructions:
Wash liver. Heat oil in large skillet. Sprinkle liver evenly with salts, accent, and pepper. Place liver in flour. Flour liver evenly on both sides. Place liver in hot oil. Cook fast until golden brown. Take liver out of oil and place on paper towel. Pour the remaining flour in oil and slice the onion and add them to flour mixture. Stir until dark brown. Return liver to flour mixture. Add 1 cup of water and cover to let simmer for 30 minutes. Stirring frequently. Serve with rice.

Serves 4.

Fairy Mississippi Rolls

1 cup margarine
2 tablespoons yeast
3/4 cup sugar
6 1/2 cups flour
2 cups water, boiled
2 egg(s)
1 teaspoon salt
1 teaspoon baking powder

Instructions:
Pour hot water over margarine and let cool. Then add yeast. Blend in 2 eggs, sugar, and salt; then flour and baking power. Mix together, then let rise for 2 hour or until doubled in size; place in warm area to do so. Then roll the dough out into round circles about 1/4 inch thick. Slice into rectangles and roll crescent rolls. Let rise again for about 2 hours. Bake for 15 minutes at 400 degrees. Brush to tops with hot butter after removing from the oven. Makes 3 1/2 to 4 dozen rolls.

Serves 4.

Fried Potatoes

6 potatoes
1 teaspoon salt
1 cup vegetable oil
1 teaspoon black pepper

Instructions:
Wash potatoes and quarter with skin on. Pour oil in large skillet. Heat until very hot. Drop potatoes in hot oil. Cook until golden brown. Remove from oil. Place on paper towel to drain. Sprinkle with salt and pepper. Serve with fried fish.

Serves 4.

Jamiya's Fast N Easy Biscuits

3/4 cup water
1 packet yeast
2 1/2 cups biscuit mix
1 cup sugar

Instructions:
Preheat oven to 350F. Combine all in ingredients in large bowl. Flour the counter top; Place mixture on it. Knead it a few times; make into balls. Spray cookie sheet with pam. Place balls on cookie sheet. Put damp rag over balls, and let stand for one hour. Then brush the top of rolls with butter. Place in oven and bake 20 to 30 minutes, or until golden brown.

Serves 4.

Scrambled Eggs with Ham

1 tablespoon butter
6 egg(s) 1/4 cup light cream
1 tablespoon chopped fresh chives
1/2 teaspoon salt
1/3 teaspoon pepper
1/3 cup ham, diced, cooked

Instructions:
Melt butter in double boiler over water. Combine eggs, cream, salt, and pepper. Beat with rotary beater until well blended. Pour into top of double boiler. Cook eggs over boiling water; stirring occasionally for 10 minutes. Add diced ham to eggs and cook, stirring several minutes longer or until eggs are of desired doneness. Stir in chives; add more salt and pepper if necessary.

DINNER

Baked Fish

3 portions haddock, skinned
1 medium onion(s)
1 can 8 oz peeled tomatoes
1 tablespoon capers
1 tablespoon chopped parsley
3 tablespoons olive oil
1 teaspoon black pepper
1 teaspoon salt
1 tablespoon celery, chopped

Instructions:
Arrange portions of haddock in a buttered shallow dish. Heat the oil and fry chopped onion gently until soft and golden brown. Add the tomatoes and seasoning. Bring to a boil and cook over a moderate heat for about 5 minutes or until the liquid is reduced to a puree. Stir in the capers, parsley, and celery; spoon the sauce even over the fish. Cover and cook for about 25 minutes. Serve hot with lemon over peas and rice.

Serves 4.

Barbecue Spareribs

4 pounds spareribs, cracked in half lengthwise
1 onion bagels, quartered
1/2 teaspoon black pepper
2 teaspoons salt

Instructions:
In large kettle, place ribs, onion, salt, and pepper in 3 quarts water. Bring to a boil. Reduce heat to simmer; cover and simmer for 1 1/2 hours or until very tender. Drain.

Barbecue Sauce: (see Barbeque Sauce recipe)
In medium saucepan; combine all ingredients for sauce. Simmer, uncovered for 1 hour; stirring occasionally. Arrange boiled spareribs on rack in broiler pan. Brush with sauce. Place in oven at 350 degrees for 30 minutes; basting frequently with sauce about every 10 minutes on each side.

Serves 4.

Big Leroy's Skillet Beef & Macaroni

1/2 pounds ground beef
2 cups elbow macaroni, uncooked
1/2 cup minced onions
1/2 cup green peppers, chopped
2 cans tomato sauce
1/2 cup sugar
1 cup water
1 teaspoon salt
1/2 teaspoon black pepper
2 tablespoons Worcestershire sauce

Instructions:
Cook beef in large skillet until it loses its redness. Remove beef from skillet. Add macaroni, onion, and green pepper to meat drippings. Cook until macaroni turns yellow. Return meat to skillet. Add tomato sauce, water, salt, sugar, pepper, and Worcestershire. Cover. Simmer 25 minutes.

Serves 4.

Boiled Pig Feet

1 package pigs' feet
1 tablespoon garlic salt
1 tablespoon seasoning salt
4 cups water I garlic cloves
1 tablespoon black pepper
1 teaspoon salt
1 onion(s)

Instructions:
Wash pig feet. Place in large pot. Add water, salts, onion, garlic, and pepper. Cover and cook over medium heat for 2 hours. Serve with beans or greens and corn bread.

Serves 4.

Braised Duck with Beer

4 pounds duck
1/4 cup fresh lemon juice
1/2 teaspoon salt
3/4 cup cooking oil
2 12 oz. bottles of beer
1/2 teaspoon cumin seed
1/2 teaspoon black pepper
2 tablespoons parsley, freshly chopped

Instructions:
If you do not know how, have the butcher cut up thawed duck in quarters. Wash duck completely and trim away excess fat. In large bowl; combine lemon and lime juice. 1/4 cup of lime juice; cumin seed, salt and pepper. Add duck and marinate over-night in refrigerator. Heat oil in heavy iron Dutch oven. Remove duck pieces from marinate. Return duck to pot. Pour in beer. Bring to rapid boil; using a wooden spoon, scrape up brown bits that cling to sides and bottom of pot. Lower heat and simmer. Cover and cook duck until tender for about 50 minutes. Place duck in quart casserole, cover and refrigerate. Then turn up heat under pot and boil down the liquid in pot until it is reduced to 3/4 cups. Cool liquid at room temperature and refrigerate until fat rises to top. Remove congealed fat and discard. About 1 hour before serving, bring stock to a boil; add duck pieces; heat thoroughly. Arrange on platter. Add stock and garnish with freshly chopped parsley.

Serves 4.

Breaded Veal Cutlet

1 package breaded veal cutlets
3 tablespoons butter
1 can mushrooms
1 teaspoon accent
1 clove garlic
2 cups wine
1/2 cup sugar
3 tablespoons olive oil
1 can tomatoes
2 teaspoons rosemary
1 onion(s)
2 beef cubes
2 teaspoons sweet basil
1 cup croutons
1 teaspoon oregano
1/2 cup parmesan cheese

Instructions:
Place veal cutlets in pan. In large bowl combine all the above ingredients. Pour over veal. Bake in oven at 350 degrees for 1 hour.

Serves 4.

Buttered Beans with Chopped Ham

1 package frozen buttered bean
1 teaspoon cornstarch
2 cups water
1 cup chopped ham, cooked
2 tablespoons sugar
1 teaspoon salt
1 teaspoon black pepper

Instructions:
In large pot place beans and water. Use 2 tbsp. water to make a paste with cornstarch and sugar. Add paste to beans. Add ham, pepper, and salt. Cover and cook over medium heat for 30 minutes.

Serves 4.

Chicken Tetrazzini

1/4 cup butter
2/3 cup parmesan cheese, shredded
1 teaspoon salt
1 package spaghetti, cooked and drained
1/2 teaspoon white pepper
2 cups half & half milk
1/2 cup sherry
1/4 teaspoon garlic salt
2 cups cooked chicken pieces
1/4 cup flour
2 chicken bouillon cubes
1 cup 3 oz sliced, boiled in butter, mushrooms; undrained

Instructions:

In large pan melt butter; blend in flour, salt, garlic salt, and pepper. Add half and half milk and bouillon cubes. Cook; stirring constantly until thick and smooth. Add sherry, 1/3 parmesan cheese, spaghetti, chicken and mushrooms; Stir carefully. Pour in shallow 2=quart casserole dish. Sprinkle with remaining parmesan cheese. Bake in moderate oven 375 degrees until hot and bubbly about 30 minutes.

Serves 4.

Collard Greens and Ham Hocks or Smoked Turkey Tail

2 bunches collard greens
2 cups water
2 teaspoons black pepper
1 package ham hock or turkey tails
1 teaspoon salt

Instructions:
Wash greens and cut each green into small pieces. In large pot put water and meat. Add greens, salt and pepper. Cover and cook for 2 hours over medium heat. Serve with cornbread.

Serves 4

Collard Greens with Neck Bones

1 1/2 pounds pork neck bones
3 bunches collard greens
1 teaspoon red peppers
1 teaspoon salt
1 teaspoon black pepper
1/2 teaspoon baking soda

Instructions:
Parboil neck bones in large saucepan. Wash greens and cut into small pieces. Add greens to the neck bones. Add black pepper, salt, red pepper, and soda. Turn heat down to low and cook until tender; about 2 hours.

Serves 4.

Corn Oysters

2 egg(s), separated
1/2 cup corn, crushed
1 tablespoon low-fat milk, lightly beaten
1/4 cup all-purpose flour
1 teaspoon sugar
1/4 teaspoon pepper
2 tablespoons cooking oil

Instructions:
Beat egg yolks in large bowl. Add corn and milk. Stir in flour, sugar and pepper. Beat egg whites until stiff peaks form. Fold into corn batter. Heat oil in large skillet on medium heat. Drop batter by tablespoonfuls into skillet. Cook about 1 1/2 minutes per side, until golden brown and puffy. Add more oil to skillet, if needed. Serve hot.

Serves 4.

Cornish Hen with Wild Rice

2 Cornish hens
1 tablespoon buffer
1 teaspoon black pepper
1 can pineapples, crushed
1 box Uncle Ben Wild Rice
1 teaspoon salt
1 teaspoon accent

Instructions:

Cook rice as directed on package. Wash hens and rub salt, pepper, and accent over entire hens with your hands. Take the butter and rub it over the ingredients with your hands last. Let hens stand for 1 hour. Stuff hens with rice; then place them in casserole dish. Add pineapples over the top of the hens. Cover and bake in oven 30 minutes. Uncover and bake 15 minutes longer at 350 degrees.

Serves 4.

Cumberland Sauce

1 cup rudy port
1/3 cup orange juice
1/2 cup red currant jelly
2 1/2 tablespoons orange peels
1 tablespoon lemon juice
1 dash canyene

Instructions:

In small saucepan, combine port, and orange peel. Cook over medium heat uncovered until reduced to 2/3 cups about 10 minutes. Stir in orange juice, lemon juice, currant jelly, and canyene until well blended. Bring to boiling; then reduce heat to simmer; uncover until jelly is melted. Serve warm or cold.

Serves 4.

Da'thy's Lobster Newburg

1/4 cup butter
2 tablespoons flour
1/2 teaspoon paprika
3 egg yolks, slightly beaten
3 cups white rice, cooked
2 cups coarsely chopped boiled lobster
1/4 teaspoon salt
1/4 teaspoon nutmeg
1 cup heavy cream
2 tablespoons sherry

Instructions:
Melt butter in top of double boiler over direct heat. Remove from heat. Stir in flour to make smooth mixture. Add salt, nutmeg, and paprika. Gradually stir in cream. Bring to boil, stirring constantly. Reduce heat and simmer; stirring 3 minutes longer. Stir a little of hot mixture into egg yolks; then pour back into top of double boiler. Add lobster and cook over hot water; stirring until mixture is thickened and lobster is hot; about 10 minutes, but do not boil. Stir in sherry. Serve over rice.

Serves 4.

Da'thy's Mississippi Baked Turkey with Oyster Stuffing

1 medium turkeys
1 tablespoon accent
1 tablespoon salt
1/2 cup butter
1 teaspoon salt
1 tablespoon black pepper

Instructions:
In roasting pan rub all ingredients on turkey with your hands. Turn turkey upside-down in pan. Cook in oven 2 hours at 350 degrees. Use Oyster Stuffing and Cornbread recipe. Take the turkey; use part of mixture for stuffing inside the turkey; Place the other around the turkey. Bake in oven at 350 degrees for 1 hour upside down; then turn turkey over and bake 1 hour more. Uncover turkey and bake 30 minutes more until brown.

Serves 4.

Da'thy's Mississippi Curry Chicken

1/2 cup butter
4 tablespoons onions, chopped
6 tablespoons flour
4 cups water
6 cups cooked chicken cubed
2 cloves garlic, minced
4 tablespoons curry powder
8 chicken bouillon cubes
1 apple pared and chopped
1 pint whipping cream

Instructions:
In large skillet melt butter, sauté onions and garlic with curry power for 5 minutes. Add flour and stir until smooth. Combine bouillon and water; slowly adding to flour mixture. Stir until thoroughly blended. Add apple and chicken; then cover and simmer for 1 hour. Add cream; bring to boil about 15 more minutes. Serve with fluffy white rice.

Serves 4.

Easy To Make Meat Loaf

1 envelope Lipton onion soup mix
2 pounds ground beef
3/4 cup plain bread crumbs
2 egg(s)
3/4 cup water
1/3 cup ketchup
1 teaspoon red peppers

Instructions:
Preheat oven to 350F. In large bowl, combine all ingredients. In a 13 by 9 inch baking or roasting pan, shape into loaf. Bake uncovered 1 hour or until done. Let stand 10 minutes before serving.

Serves 4.

Gumbo

1 whole chicken, cooked, deboned & cut-up
1 package smoked sausages, cooked & cut-up
1 pound large shrimp
1 package gumbo file
1/2 cup celery
1 teaspoon black pepper
1/4 cup vegetable oil
6 cups water
1 can tomatoes, peeled
2 bay leaves
1/2 cup onions, chopped
1 teaspoon salt
1/2 cup flour
8 crab legs
1 package okra, frozen

Instructions:

In large pot make a rue with flour and oil. To make rue add flour and oil together. Brown until dark. Add celery, onion, and gumbo file. Cook until vegetables are tender. Add water, tomatoes, okra, bay leaves, salt and pepper. Cook over medium heat 15 minutes. Add shrimp, and crab legs. Cook 15 minutes. Add sausages and chicken. Cook 10 minutes. Serve with rice.

Serves 4.

Honey Baked Ham

1 ham
1 cup honey
1 box brown sugar
1/3 cup mustard

Instructions:
Insert meat thermometer in center of ham away from bone. Mix brown sugar, honey and mustard; pat mixture on ham. Place ham in center of 3-quart shallow baking dish or shallow casserole. Bake in oven at 350 degrees for one hour or until meat thermometer register 130 degrees.

Serves 4.

Lemon Chicken

3 pounds boneless chicken breast
1 tablespoon soy sauce
2 egg(s)
1/2 teaspoon baking powder
1/2 teaspoon sherry
1 1/2 teaspoons salt
1/3 cup cornstarch
2 1/4 cups vegetable oil
1/3 cup sugar
1 cup chicken broth
1 lemons, thinly sliced
1 tablespoon lemon juice

Instructions:

Combine chicken with sherry, soy sauce and 1/2 teaspoon salt. Marinate for about one hour. Beat eggs, add cornstarch and baking powder to form a smooth batter. Heat oil to 350 degrees. Coat chicken with batter and fry until brown. Cut chicken into 1x1x1/2 inch pieces and arrange on a serving platter.

Sauce:

Combine sugar, 1 tablespoon of cornstarch, broth, lemon juice, and 1 teaspoon salt. Heat remaining oil. Stir-fry the lemon slices for 30 seconds. Slowly stir in cornstarch mixture. Cook stirring constantly until sauce is clear. Pour over chicken and serve immediately.

Serves 4.

Meatballs N Gravy

2 cans mushroom soup
2 pounds hamburger meat

Instructions:
In a large bowl place the meat. Make small meatballs about 1 1/2 inches wide. Spray frying pan with Pam. Place meatballs in pan to fry. When they are well done add the mushroom soup but do not drain the grease. Do not add any water or milk. Stir soup in until it blends completely with the grease. Then turn heat down to simmer; simmer for 10 minutes. Serve over whipped potatoes. Hot buttered corn is an excellent side dish.

Serves 4.

Mississippi Fried Steak and Gravy

1 round steak
1/2 cup flour
2 teaspoons seasoning salt
1 teaspoon black pepper
1 onion(s)
1 teaspoon salt
1 teaspoon garlic powder
1/3 cup vegetable oil

Instructions:

Clean and cut-up steak. Place oil in large frying pan. Chop onion. Sprinkle salts, pepper, and garlic power evenly over meat. Dip meat in flour and fry in oil until golden brown. Place meat on paper towel. Pour flour in pan. Brown with grease from cooking steak. Then return meat to mixture. Add onions and 1 cup water. Cover and simmer for 30 minutes. Serve with rice.

Serves 4.

Mississippi Hearty Beef Stew

1 package stew beef
1/2 cup green peppers
1 teaspoon salt
3 potatoes, diced
1 package cut corn
3 cups water
1 onions, chopped
1/2 cup celery
1 teaspoon black pepper
3 carrots, cut-up
1 can tomatoes, peeled
1 teaspoon seasoning salt

Instructions:
In large pot place all the above items. Cook over low heat covered for 3 hours. Serve with cornbread.

Serves 4.

Mississippi Smothered Rabbit with Gravy

1 package rabbits
1 teaspoon black pepper
1 cup vegetable oil
1 teaspoon accent
1 teaspoon salt
1 teaspoon seasoning salt
1 cup flour
3 cups water

Instructions:
Boil rabbit in 2 cups water over medium heat for 30 minutes. Take out of water and cool. Place on paper towel. Sprinkle with accent, salts, and pepper. Pour oil in large skillet. Coat rabbit in flour. Place in oil and fry until golden brown. Take out of oil, and place on paper towel. Pour the flour from coating the rabbit in the oil that the rabbit was cooked in. Brown the flour until dark brown. Add 1 cup water and return rabbit to skillet. Cover and simmer for 30 minutes. Serve with rice.

Serves 4.

Mississippi Smothered Steak

1 round steak, cut-up
1 tablespoon seasoning salt
1/3 cup vegetable oil
1/2 cup flour
1 teaspoon black pepper
1 teaspoon salt
1 onion(s)
2 cups water

Instructions:
Wash meat. Sprinkle salts, and pepper evenly over meat. Let stand one hour. In large fry pan pour oil. Place over medium heat. Coat meat in flour. Place in hot oil. Cook for 30 minutes or until golden brown. Gravy: 1 small onion, flour from steak, 2 cups water. Place flour from dripping of steak in pan. Slice onion and brown with flour. Stir until dark brown. Return steak and add water. Cover and simmer 30 minutes. Serve with rice.

Serves 4.

Mixed Greens

3 bunches turnips
2 teaspoons salt
1 package salt pork
2 teaspoons black pepper
4 cups water
3 bunches Texas mustard

Instructions:

In large pot place water and pork. Cook over medium heat covered for 2 hours. Meantime pick and wash greens. Wash green several times. Add greens to pot; Add 1/2 salt and pepper. Cook over medium heat for 1 1/2 hours. If needed add the remaining salt. Serve with cornbread.

Serves 4.

Oven Fried Chicken

3 pounds broiler fryers, cut-up
1/8 teaspoon black pepper
3/4 teaspoon salt
3 tablespoons flour
3/4 teaspoon paprika
1/4 cup butter

Instructions:
Preheat oven at 425 degrees. Wash and dry chicken well with paper towels. Combine flour mixture. In shallow baking pan melt butter in oven. Remove from oven. Arrange chicken in pan in single layer, skin side down. Bake uncovered for 30 minutes. With tongs, turn chicken and bake 15 minutes longer or until brown and fork-tender. Serve with Cumberland sauce.

Serves 4.

Pineapple Duck

5 pounds duck quartered
2 tablespoons honey
1 teaspoon orange peels, grated
1/4 cup wine vinegar
1 cup pineapple chunks
3 teaspoons cornstarch
3 tablespoons cold water
1 tablespoon salt
3 tablespoons soy sauce
1/2 cup orange juice
1/2 teaspoon onion powder

Instructions:
Preheat oven to 450 degrees. Remove any visible fat from duck; sprinkle duck with salt. Roast for 30 minutes. Combine honey, soy sauce, orange juice, orange peel, vinegar, and onion power. Transfer duck to shallow baking pan. Coat with half of the sauce and bake for an additional 45 minutes; basting frequently. Add pineapple chunks to remainder of sauce and heat. Combine cornstarch with water; stir into sauce. Bring to a boil. Serve with rice.

Serves 4.

Pinto Beans and Ham Hocks

1 16 oz. can pinto beans
6 cups water
1 onions, chopped
1 tablespoon seasoning salt
1 package ham hocks
2 teaspoons black pepper
1 teaspoon salt

Instructions:

Rinse and salt beans. In a large pot soak beans with 2 cups of hot water for 2 to 4 hours. Add remaining water, ham hocks, pepper, salts and onion. Cover and cook over medium heat for 2 hours. Serve with cornbread.

Serves 4.

Pork Chitterlings

1 pail chitterlings
1 garlic cloves
1 teaspoon salt
8 cups water
1 onion(s)
1 tablespoon black pepper
1 tablespoon seasoning salt
1 potatoes

Instructions:
Let chitterling stand on sink overnight. Take each chitterling and clean excess fat. Then run water over each chitterling. Place chitterling in large pot with 4 cups water. Cover and boil for 2 hours. Place the potato on top of pot, so the smell is cut. Then take the chitterlings and drain all the water from them. Place the chitterling on the side and wash the pot. Add 4 cups of water, chitterling, onion, salts, garlic, and pepper. Return to heat and cook over medium heat another 2 hours.

Serves 4.

Pork Neck Bones and Black Eyes Peas

1 package neck bones
1 teaspoon black pepper
6 cups water
1 small onions, chopped
1 teaspoon garlic salt
1 teaspoon salt
1 tablespoon seasoning salt
1 package 16 oz black eyes peas

Instructions:
Rinse and soak peas in a large pot with cups of water for 4 hours. Add the other water and all the items mentioned above. Cook over medium heat for 2 hours. Serve with corn bread.

Serves 4.

Roast Hen with Stuffing

1 capons
3 teaspoons accent
2 tablespoons butter
2 teaspoons black pepper
2 tablespoons seasoning salt
3 egg(s), beaten
6 slices white bread, toasted
1 small onions, chopped
1 cup celery, chopped
2 tablespoons poultry seasoning
4 cups cornbread
1 pound giblets

Instructions:
Wash hen. Rub hen with pepper, accent, and salt; then rub with butter; set aside for about 2 hours. **Stuffings:** Boil giblets until tender; cool. Cut up into small pieces. Add cornbread, eggs, and toast. Sauté onion, pepper, celery, then add to mixture; add poultry seasoning; then stuff hen with stuffing. The extra stuffing should be placed in the pan on the sides of the hen. Cover hen in roasting pan and place in oven at 350 degrees for 2 hours.

Serves 4.

Sweet and Sour Meatballs

1 pound lean ground beef
3/4 cup celery, minced
1/4 cup almonds, chopped
1 clove garlic, minced
1/2 teaspoon black pepper
1 teaspoon salt
1/2 cup soft bread crumbs
2 1/2 tablespoons soy sauce
2 egg(s), slightly beaten
3/4 cup green peppers, chopped
1 can chicken bouillon
1/2 cup sugar
3 tablespoons cornstarch
1 can pineapple chunks
1/2 cup pineapple juice
1/2 cup vinegar

Instructions:
In large bowl, thoroughly mix all ingredients (lean ground beef, celery, almonds, garlic, black pepper, salt, bread crumbs, soy sauce, and eggs.) Form into small meatballs. Brown meatballs and drain on paper towels.

Sauce:
In a saucepan, add bouillon, sugar, cornstarch, pineapple juice, vinegar, and 2 tsp. soy sauce. Over medium heat, stir for 3 minutes or until thickened. Add green peppers, pineapple chunks, and meatballs; then bake in oven for 30 minutes.

Serves 4.

Turkey Parts with Rice

1 package turkey wings, tails, or necks.
1 onion(s)
1/2 cup green peppers
1 teaspoon black pepper
1 teaspoon garlic salt
1/3 cup butter
1/2 cup celery
1 tablespoon seasoning salt
1 teaspoon salt
1 cup rice, uncooked
4 cups water

Instructions:
In large pot place turkey parts and water. Add onion; chopped, celery, salts, and pepper. Cook covered over medium heat for 30 minutes. Add rice and butter. Cook 15 minutes. Let stand 15 minutes covered. Then serve. Serve with corn bread.

Serves 4.

Veal with Sauce

9 ounces veal, thinly sliced
1 teaspoon salt
2 tablespoons butter
2 ounces fresh mushrooms, sliced
1/2 cup whipping cream
1 teaspoon white pepper
2 tablespoons flour
1 tablespoon onion(s), finely chopped
1/4 cup white wine
1 cup brown sauce

Instructions:
Put veal in pan. Sprinkle with salt and white pepper. Sprinkle with flour. Quickly sauté in butter until slightly browned on all sides. Remove veal. Add onions and mushrooms and sauté for 1 minute. Add white wine, cream and brown sauce; then simmer for another minute. Add veal to sauce. Heat thoroughly, but do not boil. Sprinkle with chopped parsley. Serve with potatoes.

DESSERT

Apple Pie

1 teaspoon nutmeg
2 pounds apples, peeled
3 tablespoons sugar

Instructions:
Use pie crust recipe.

Filling for Apple Pie:
1 lb. tart apples peeled, 1 lb. eating apples peeled, cored, and sliced thinly. 1 tbsp. nutmeg sugar to taste

Preheat oven to 425 degrees. Heat a baking sheet. Roll out a little more than half of crust and line a greased 9 inch pie pan. Pile apples onto pan. Add nutmeg and about 3 tablespoon sugar; exact amount will depend on apples used. Use rest of crust to form a lid. Dampen edge of base with water and put lid on top of pie. Flute edge and make steam slits. Glaze with reserved egg and sprinkle with confectioner's sugar. Bake on hot baking sheet for about 30 minutes. Serve with ice cream.

Serves 4.

Banana Nut Bread

2 1/2 cups all-purpose flour
1/2 cup brown sugar
3 1/2 teaspoons baking powder
1 teaspoon salt
3 tablespoons vegetable oil
1/3 cup milk
1 egg(s)
1 tablespoon orange juice
1 teaspoon orange peels, grated
1 1/4 bananas, mashed
1/2 cup sugar

Instructions:
Heat oven to 350F. Mix all ingredients; beat 30 seconds. Use a 9 inch loaf pan. Spray bottom with pam baking oil. Pour into pan. Bake for 65 to 70 minutes.

Serves 4.

Chocolate Pound Cake

1 cup water, boiled
2 squares sweetened chocolate, cut-up
2 cups all-purpose flour, sifted
1/2 cup buffer, room temperature
1 teaspoon vanilla
1/2 cup dairy sour cream, defrosted
2 egg(s)
1 teaspoon baking soda
1/4 teaspoon salt
1 1/2 cups light brown sugar
1/4 cup confectionary sugar

Instructions:
In small bowl; pour boiling water over chocolate. Let stand 20 minutes to cool. Meanwhile; preheat oven to 325 degrees. Grease well and flour 9x5x3 inch loaf pan. Sift flour, baking soda, and salt together. In large bowl with electric mixer at high speed, beat butter, brown sugar, eggs and vanilla until light and fluffy. At low speed beat in flour mixture, in fourths, alternately with sour cream. Beat in cooled chocolate. Pour into prepared pan; bake 1 hour. Cool in pan on wire rack; 15 minutes. Transfer from pan to rack; cool completely. Sprinkle with confectionery sugar.

Serves 4.

Cottage Cheese Jell-O Salad

1 1/2 cups cottage cheese
1 small tub cool whip
1 can mandarin oranges, drained
1 package orange flavoured Jell-O
1 can pineapples, crushed

Instructions:

Thaw cool whip; place in bowl; stir in Jell-O until dissolved. Add cottage cheese, drained crushed pineapples, and mandarin oranges. Mix well and chill until firm; approximately 1 hour.

Serves 4.

Da'thy's Can't Get Enough Peach Cobbler

1 can sliced peaches
1 tablespoon vanilla
1 1/2 tablespoons nutmeg
1 stick butter
1 box Betty Cooker Pie Crust Mix
1 egg(s)
1 tablespoon allspice
1 teaspoon cinnamon
2 cups sugar

Instructions:

Prepare pie crust as directed on package and place in oven for 10 minutes. In large sauce pan combine peaches, egg, vanilla, allspice, nutmeg, cinnamon, butter and sugar. Cook over low heat 15 minutes until blended well. Pour into shell. Place pie crust on top sprinkle with sugar. Place in oven. Cook 1 hour at 350 degrees.

Serves 4.

Da'thy's Can't Stop Eat'em Candie Yams

4 large yams peeled and cut-up
1 small box powdered sugar
1 tablespoon cinnamon
1 tablespoon allspice
2 sticks butter
2 tablespoons vanilla
2 tablespoons nutmeg
2 cups water

Instructions:
In large pot place yams and water. Cover over medium heat for 15 minutes. Add sugar and butter. Mix cinnamon, allspice, and nutmeg together. Add to pot. Cook 15 minutes. Add vanilla cook 30 more minutes over low heat with pot covered.

Serves 4.

Da'thy's Mississippi Pound Cake

3 cups gold medal flour
2 teaspoons baking powder
2 cups sugar
3 egg yolks
1/4 teaspoon salt
1/2 cup sweet butter
1 cup plain yogurt
1 teaspoon vanilla

Instructions:
Cream butter and sugar together beating for 10 minutes. Add egg yolks one at a time; Add flour, yogurt, and egg whites. Pour in greased pan. Bake at 350 degrees for 1 hour.

Serves 4.

Da'thy's Mouth Watering Sweet Potato Pie

4 sweet potatoes
1 small Pet evaporated Milk
1 1/2 cups sugar
1 teaspoon cinnamon
3 egg(s)
4 cups water
2 pie shells
1 tablespoon nutmeg
1 tablespoon allspice
1 tablespoon vanilla

Instructions:
In large pot add potatoes and water. Cook over medium heat until potatoes are soft. Take out of water. Let stand until cool. Peel potatoes and place in mixing bowl. Add milk and sugar. Beat well. Add eggs, nutmeg, allspice, vanilla, and cinnamon. Blend well. Pour into 2 pie shells and place in oven at 350 degrees for 1 hour.

Serves 4.

German Sweet Chocolate Cake

1 package
4 oz Baker German Sweet Chocolate
1/2 cup water, boiled
2 cups sugar
1 teaspoon vanilla
2 1/2 cups sifted Swans Down Cake Flour
1 teaspoon baking soda
1 cup buttermilk
1 cup butter
1/2 teaspoon salt
4 egg whites, stiffly beaten
4 egg yolks

Instructions:
Melt chocolate in boiling water; cool. Cream butter and sugar together until fluffy. Add yolks; one at a time; beating well after each; blend in vanilla and chocolate. Sift flour with soda, and salt. Add buttermilk to chocolate mixture; beating until smooth. Fold in beaten whites. Pour into 3 8 or 9 inch layer pans; lined on bottoms with paper. Bake at 350 for 30 to 40 minutes; Cool. Frost tops only.

Serves 4.

Ginger Cookies

1 cup shortening
1 cup sugar
1 egg(s), beaten
1/4 cup molasses
2 cups flour
1 teaspoon salt
1 teaspoon ginger
1 teaspoon cloves
1 teaspoon cinnamon
1 teaspoon baking soda

Instructions:
Cream shortening, egg, sugar, and molasses. Add all dry ingredients. Do not add too much flour to cutting board; place dough to flour and roll out and cut. Bake at 350F for 10 minutes.

Serves 4.

Hoe Cakes

1/4 cup oil
1 1/2 cups self-rising cornmeal
1/4 teaspoon baking soda
1 1/4 cups buttermilk
1 egg(s), lightly beaten
1 tablespoon Crisco Shortening, melted

Instructions:

Heat 1/4 oil to 365F in heavy skillet. Combine cornmeal and baking soda in medium bowl. Add buttermilk, egg and on tablespoon melted shortening. Stir just until dry ingredients are moistened. Pour 1/4 cup batter into skillet for each hoe cake. Fry 1 or 2 minutes or until golden brown on each side. Add additional shortening, if necessary. Drain on paper towels. Serve immediately.

Serves 4.

Jell-O Lemon Pudding Cake

1 package Jell-O lemon instant pudding and pie filling
1 package lemon or yellow cake mix
1 cup water
4 egg(s)
1/4 cup oil

Instructions:
Blend all ingredients in large mixing bowl; beat 2 minutes at medium speed. Bake in greased and floured 10 inch tube pan at 350 degrees for 1 hour. Bake until done. Remove from pan.

Serves 4.

Kentucky Bourbon Sweet Potatoes

3 cans sweet potatoes, drained
1 cup sugar
1/3 cup bourbon
1/2 cup butter
1/2 teaspoon vanilla extract
2 cups miniature marshmallows

Instructions:
Preheat oven 350F. Turn sweet potatoes into large saucepan. Cook over medium heat, stirring frequently, until heated through. Mash sweet potatoes. Add sugar, bourbon, butter, and vanilla; beat until well blended. Turn into 2-quart, shallow baking dish. Sprinkle marshmallows over top. Bake, uncovered, 30 minutes, or until marshmallows are golden brown.

Serves 4.

Lime Pie

1/2 cup soften butter
1 teaspoon vanilla
1 14 oz. can condensed milk, sweetened
1/2 cup lime juice
1/4 teaspoon vanilla
1 cup confectionary sugar
1 1/2 cups graham crackers, crumbled
6 egg(s)
2 teaspoons lime rind, grated
1 teaspoon cream of tartar

Instructions:

To make crust: Blend butter with crumbled crackers. Add 1/4 tsp vanilla. Spread and press mixture around bottom and sides of a 9 inch pie pan.

To make filling: Blend egg yolks with milk. Add lime juice. Put filling into pie crust. Bake for 15 minutes at 350 degrees.

To make meringue: Beat egg whites until frothy. Add vanilla, cream of tartar, and salt. Beat slightly. Add sugar gradually, beating well until mixture forms stiff peaks. Swirl over pie filling and bake at 400 degrees for 10 minutes, or until the meringue is browned. Allow to cool and refrigerate before serving.

Serves 4.

Mississippi Banana Pudding

1 cup sugar
3 tablespoons cornstarch
1 dash salt
2 cups carnation milk, canned
4 egg(s)
2 tablespoons butter
2 teaspoons vanilla extract
85 vanilla wafers
5 bananas, sliced

Instructions:
Preheat oven to 400F. In medium saucepan, combine sugar, cornstarch, and salt; gradually add milk. Cook over medium heat until mixture come to a boil, stirring constantly. Continue to boil 3 minutes, stirring constantly. Remove from heat. Place egg yolks in medium bowl, then mash 2 of the bananas, gradually stir in milk mixture. Return mixture to saucepan. Cook over medium heat until mixture returns to a boil, stirring constantly. Continue to boil 2 minutes, stirring constantly. Remove from heat. Add butter and vanilla, mix well. In 1 1/2 quart round baking dish layer half of wafers, then put half of the bananas, then half of the pudding. Now add the other wafers, then other bananas, and the rest of the pudding. In medium bowl beat egg whites to soft peak. Gradually add 1h cup sugar, beat until stiff. Spread over pudding. Bake 10 minutes or until golden brown.

Serves 4.

Mississippi Pecan Pie

1 cup Crisco
1/4 cup butter
3/4 cup maple or corn syrup
1/2 cup dark brown sugar
1 1/2 cups flour
1/4 cup soften butter
3 tablespoons cold water
3 egg(s)
1 tablespoon milk
1 pinch of salt
1/2 teaspoon vanilla
1 cup halved pecan

Instructions:
Crust:

Sift flour and salt. Rub Crisco coarsely into flour with fingertips, leaving flakes of Crisco throughout. Stir in sufficient cold water to form a dough, knead lightly, then wrap in foil and chill until firm. Preheat oven to 425 degrees. Roll out pastry and line a 9 inch pie pan. Flute edge and chill. Beat eggs and milk together. Boil syrup and sugar together for 3 minutes. Slowly pour into beaten eggs. Stir in butter and vanilla. Use half of nuts to cover bottom of pie shell. Spoon syrup mixture and cover the nuts; then cover the top with remaining nuts. Bake 10 minutes. Reduce heat to 325 degrees and cook 45 minutes longer until filling is set.

Serves 4.

Molasses Brown Bread

1 egg(s), lightly beaten
1 cup all-bran or bran bud cereal
1/2 cup raisins
1/3 cup molasses
2 tablespoons butter flavour Crisco
3/4 cup water, boiling
1 cup all-purpose flour
1 teaspoon baking soda
1/2 teaspoon cinnamon

Instructions:
Heat oven to 350F. Grease inside of two clean metal food cans, with labels removed. (41/2 inches deep X 3 inches wide.) Combine egg, cereal, raisins, molasses, and Crisco in large mixing bowl. Add hot water, stirring until shortening is melted. Combine flour, baking soda and cinnamon. Add to cereal mixture, stirring just until combined. Fill cans two-thirds full. Bake at 350F for 45 minutes or until toothpick inserted in center comes out clean. Remove from cans. Cool slightly. Slice and serve warm or cool completely on cooling rack. Wrap tightly when cooled. Make 2 loaves.

Serves 4.

Peanut Butter Bon Bars

1 can Pillsbury ready to spread vanilla frosting supreme
1 can Pillsbury ready to spread chocolate fudge frosting supreme
1 cup peanut butter
1/2 cup butter, softened
2 cups graham crackers, crumbs

Instructions:

In large bowl, combine vanilla frosting, peanut butter, and butter with fork until well blended. Stir in crumbs until well mixed. Form into one inch balls. Chill one hour. In small saucepan, melt chocolate frosting over low heat, stirring occasionally. Dip chilled balls in melted frosting. Allow excess to drip off. Place on cooling rack over waxed paper, about 6 hours. Store in a cool and dry place. Make 5 dozen bon bars.

Serves 4.

Pie Crust

1/2 cup white Crisco, diced
1 1/2 cups all-purpose flour
3 tablespoons water, ice cold
1/2 cup butter
1 teaspoon salt

Instructions:
Sift flour and salt together. Rub Crisco coarsely into flour with fingertips, leaving flakes of Crisco throughout. Stir in sufficient cold water to form a dough, knead lightly, then wrap in foil and chill until firm.

Serves 4.

Pumpkin Pie

1 pound pumpkins
1/2 cup sugar
1 teaspoon flour
1 tablespoon milk
1 cup whole blanched almonds skinned
1 teaspoon orange juice
1 egg(s)

Instructions:
Cut off pumpkin akin and remove seeds. Cut-up flesh and place in a saucepan with 3 tablespoons of water. Cover and cook over low heat until softened. Puree pumpkin, return to pan, and cook over low heat, until thick and smooth. Transfer to a bowl. Boil almonds until pale and golden. Crush in blender with sugar and orange juice. Stir into pumpkin puree. Preheat oven to 425 degrees. Roll out 9 oz pie shell. Spread pumpkin mixture evenly over crust (see Pie Crust recipe). Use part of crust to make top on pie. Make a stripped top. Bake 35 minutes.

Serves 4.

Sautéed Bananas

2 cups oil
2 tablespoons orange juice
4 firm ripe bananas
2 tablespoons confectionary sugar

Instructions:
Melt oil in large skillet on medium heat. Stir in orange juice. Peel bananas. Cut in half crosswise and then lengthwise. Place in skillet. Cook 5 minutes, turning once. Arrange bananas in serving dish. Sprinkle with confectioners' sugar. Serve hot for dessert.

LUNCH

Buttermilk Hush Puppies

1 Crisco oil
1 cup yellow cornmeal
1/2 cup all-purpose flour
1 1/2 teaspoons baking soda
1/2 teaspoon salt
1 cup buttermilk
1 egg(s), beaten
1 cup onion(s), finely chopped

Instructions:
Heat 2 to 3 inches Crisco to 365F in deep fryer or deep saucepan. Combine cornmeal, flour, baking soda, and salt in large bowl. Stir in buttermilk, egg and onion. Mix well. Drop by teaspoon, a few at a time, into Crisco. Fry 2 minutes or until dark brown. Turn as needed for even browning. Remove with metal spoon. Drain on paper towels. Serve immediately.

Serves 4.

Chicken Casserole

1 ²/³ cups carrots, thinly sliced
2 tablespoons buffer
1/4 cup onions, diced
2 cups 2 cups chicken stock or 2 bouillon cubes dissolved in 2 cups of water
1 ¹/³ cups instant rice
2 teaspoons sugar
1 teaspoon salt
1 package frozen green peas
1 tablespoon flour
1/2 teaspoon poultry seasoning

Instructions:

In a large skillet sauté carrots in butter until almost tender; turning frequently about 10 minutes. Add onions and sauté until tender. Stir in flour; blending well. Add remaining ingredients except chicken, rice, and peas. Bring to a boil. Stir in peas, chicken, and rice. Cover and simmer for 10 minutes.

Serves 4.

Chicken Gizzards with Rice

1 package chicken gizzards
1/2 cup onions, chopped
1/2 cup green peppers
1 tablespoon seasoning salt
1 tablespoon garlic salt
1 can cream of chicken soup
1 cup rice
1/2 cup celery
1/2 stick butter
1 teaspoon salt
1 teaspoon black pepper
6 cups water

Instructions:
Clean gizzards by taking off fat and yellow skin. Wash. In large pot place water. Sprinkle gizzards evenly with salts and pepper. Put into water. Add onions, green peppers, and celery. Cook over medium heat for 45 minutes, Add soup, butter and rice cook 15 minutes. Turn off heat and let stand 15 minutes. Do not overcook. It should have thick sauce. Serve with corn bread.

Serves 4.

Chicken with Biscuit Crisps

3 whole chicken breasts, halved
1/4 cup onions, chopped
1/2 cup celery, finely chopped
1/8 tablespoon black pepper
21 tablespoons flour
2 tablespoons butter
2 tablespoons salt
1 cup water
1 cup skim milk

Instructions:
Simmer chicken; covered with onion, celery, salt, pepper and water in a medium size frying pan 30 minutes or until tender. Remove to heated serving platter; keep hot while making gravy.

Gravy:
Mix flour and skim milk in a cup. Stir into hot broth in pan. Cook; stirring constantly until gravy thickens and boils 1 minute. Serve in a separate bowel or spoon over chicken and split hot biscuit crisps.

Biscuit Crisps:
Combine 1 cup sifted regular flour, 1 1/2 tsp baking powder and 1/4 tsp salt in a medium size bowl. Cut in 2 tsp butter with a pastry blender until mixture is crumbly. Add 1/3 cup skim milk all at once; stir lightly with a fork just until mixture is evenly moist. Turn out onto a lightly floured pastry cloth or board; knead gently; flouring hands lightly 5 or 6 times; then pat into a rectangle about 1/2 inch thick; cut into 6 squares.

Place on a lightly-greased cookie sheet. Brush tops with skim milk.

Bake in hot oven 425 degrees for 10 to 12 minutes or until lightly browned. Break apart with forks for serving.

Serves 4.

Chili

1 pound ground beef or turkey
1 package chili seasonings
2 cups pinto beans, cooked
2 cans beer
1 onions, chopped
1 can diced tomatoes

Instructions:
In large skillet, brown meat until crumbly; drain fat. Add seasoning, beer, beans, onions, and tomatoes. Bring to a boil, reduce heat to low and cook covered for 1 hour; stirring occasionally.

Serves 4.

Chili Tacos

1/2 pound lean ground beef
1/2 cup green peppers, chopped
2 teaspoons chili powder
1/4 teaspoon cumin seed
1/2 teaspoon celery seed
1 can 5.8 oz whole kernel corn, drained
3 drops hot pepper sauce
1/8 ounce tomato soup, canned
3/4 cup refried beans
1/2 cup onions, chopped
1 clove garlic, minced
1/2 teaspoon oregano, crumbled

Instructions:

Crumble ground beef in saucepan. Add chopped onion. Garlic and green pepper. Cover and cook for 10 minutes over medium heat. Stirring occasionally. Drain off fat and liquid. Stir in chili powder. Cumin seed, celery seed, oregano, corn, hot pepper sauce, tomato sauce, and refried beans. Cover and let cook for 15 minutes. Stirring occasionally.

NOTE: Serve on a crisp tortilla or with corn chips. As filling for crepes or as omelettes, or place on crisp lettuce leaves then roll and eat.

Serves 4.

Pineapple Chicken

3 pounds chicken fryers, cut-up
3/4 teaspoon paprika
3/4 teaspoon salt
3 tablespoons flour
1 teaspoon black pepper
1/4 cup cooking oil

Instructions:
Wash and dry chicken well with paper towels. Combine flour, paprika, salt, pepper. Coat chicken with flour mixture. In frying pan heat oil. Fry chicken in oil until brown. Remove chicken from oil and place on paper towel. Then place chicken in shallow roasting pan; arranging pieces skin inside. Then preheat oven to 350 degrees;

Pineapple Sauce: (see pineapple sauce recipe)

Boil 2 minutes; pour over chicken. Bake uncovered for 30 minutes. Add pineapple slices and green pepper; Bake 30 minutes longer or until chicken is tender. Serve with fluffy white rice.

Serves 4.

Da'thy's Quick Chicken and Dumplings

1 whole chicken cut-up
1 can cream of mushroom soup
1 package Pillsbury buttermilk biscuits
1/2 cup celery
4 cups water
2 teaspoons salt
2 teaspoons accent
1 teaspoon black pepper
1/2 cup green peppers

Instructions:
In large pot place water, rinse chicken; sprinkle with accent, salt and pepper. Add chicken to water. Add celery, soup, and peppers. Cook for 30 minutes. Then roll the biscuits out and cut into small pieces; place them in pot cook another 15 minutes.

Serves 4.

Da'thy's Mississippi Fried Chicken

1 whole chicken fryers, cut-up
2 teaspoons garlic powder
2 teaspoons seasoning salt
2 cups vegetable oil
2 teaspoons accent
2 egg(s), beaten
1/2 tablespoon black pepper
2 large brown grocery bags doubled for extra thickness
2 teaspoons salt

Instructions:
Rinse chicken and pat dry. Pour vegetable oil in large black cast iron skillet and heat. Sprinkle chicken evenly with salt, pepper, accent, garlic power, and seasoned salt. Dip chicken in beaten eggs. Put flour inside of brown bags; then place the chicken pieces into the bag; then shake until flour is all over the chicken pieces. Place chicken in hot oil and cover. Cook over medium heat until golden brown. Take out of oil and place the chicken on paper towels. Arrange on platter before serving.

Serves 4.

Da'thy's Sock-It-To-Me Baked Macaroni and Cheese

1 package elbow macaroni
1 teaspoon salt
1 package 8 oz. cheddar cheese
1/2 cup sugar
3 egg(s), beaten
2 teaspoons black pepper
1 package 8 oz Monterey jack cheese
1/3 cup milk

Instructions:
Cook macaroni as directed on package and drain. Let cool. Add eggs, salt, and pepper blend well. Grate cheeses then add to mixture. Stir in sugar and milk blend well. Pour into baking dish and sprinkle top with cheese. Place in oven at 350 degrees for 1 hour.

Serves 4.

Da'thy's Fast Chili

1 pound ground beef or turkey
1 package chili seasonings
2 cups pinto beans, cooked
2 cans beer
1 onion(s), chopped
1 can diced tomatoes

Instructions:
In large skillet brown meat until crumbly; drain fat. Add seasoning, beer, beans, onions, and tomatoes. Bring to a boil. Reduce heat to low and cook covered for 1 hour; stirring occasionally.

Serves 4.

Da'thy's Quick Meatloaf

1 pound ground beef or turkey
1 teaspoon salt
2 teaspoons black pepper
3/4 cup oatmeal, uncooked
1 small onion(s)
1 teaspoon accent
2 egg(s), beaten
1 teaspoon seasoning salt

Instructions:
Chopped onion. Mix all other ingredients well together with your hands. Add onions. Shape in a loaf in a baking pan. Bake at 350 degrees for 1 hour until brown.

Serves 4.

Fried Cat Fish Nuggets

1 package cat fish nuggets
1 teaspoon salt
1 teaspoon red peppers
1 egg(s)
1/2 cup water
1 cup vegetable oil
2 teaspoons black pepper
1 teaspoon seasoning salt
1 cup yellow cornmeal

Instructions:
Rinse cat fish. Preheat oil in large frying pan. Sprinkle all dry ingredients evenly over fish. In a small bowl combine egg and water blend in corn meal to make a batter. Dip the fish in the batter and place in hot oil. Cook until golden brown.

Serves 4.

Fried Chicken Gizzards

1/2 cup flour
1 package chicken gizzards
1 teaspoon salt
1/2 cup vegetable oil
1 tablespoon garlic salt
1 teaspoon black pepper
2 egg(s)
1 tablespoon seasoning salt

Instructions:
Clean gizzards by taking off fat and yellow skin. Wash. Place gizzards on paper towels. Sprinkle with salts and pepper evenly. In large skillet, pour oil. Heat. Make a batter with eggs and flour. Dip gizzards in batter and drop in hot oil. Fry until golden brown.

Serves 4.

Fried Fish

1 pound catfish or red snapper
1 tablespoon seasoning salt
1 cup vegetable oil
2 tablespoons flour
1 teaspoon salt
1 teaspoon black pepper
1 cup yellow cornmeal

Instructions:
Clean fish. Place on paper towel. Sprinkle evenly with salts and pepper. Let stand. In large frying skillet pour oil. Heat over medium heat until very hot. Sift flour and cornmeal together. Coat fish in mixture. Drop in hot oil. Cook fast until golden brown. Remove from oil and place on paper towel to drain.

Serves 4.

Jessie Palmer's Bake Burgers

2 pounds ground beef
1/2 cup tomato sauce
1 onion(s), cut-up
6 sliced bread, cubed
1 tablespoon garlic salt
1 tablespoon black pepper
1 teaspoon red peppers

Instructions:
Pre heat oven to 350F. In large bowl, combine everything together by hand. Shape into 8 patties. Place in a skillet; put in over and bake uncovered 1 hour or until done. Let stand 10 minutes before serving

Serves 4.

Sausage Rice Casserole

1 pound sausages
1 can cream of mushroom soup
1 can cream of chicken soup
1 can cream of celery soup
1 cup water

Instructions:
Heat oven to 350F. Crumble sausage into medium skillet. Brown on medium heat. Drain. Spoon into 2-quart casserole. Add rice, mushroom soup, chicken soup, celery soup, and water. Stir well. Bake 350F for 30 to 40 minutes, stirring after 25 minutes. Bake until rice is tender.

Serves 4.

Summer Squash Casserole

2 pounds Zucchini or yellow squash, about 6 cups sliced
1/4 cup onions, chopped
1 dash salt
1 can cream of chicken soup
1 cup sour cream
1 cup shredded carrot
1 package herb seasoned stuffing mix
1/2 cup melted butter

Instructions:
Heat oven to 350F: Combine squash and onion in large saucepan. Cover with water. Season with salt. Cook 5 minutes. Drain. Combine soup and sour cream in large bowl. Stir in carrots. Fold in squash and onions. Combine stuffing mix and butter. Spread half into bottom of 12 x 7 1/2 x 2 inch baking dish. Spoon in vegetable mixture. Sprinkle with remaining stuffing. Bake at 350F for 30 minutes or until heated thoroughly.

SIDE

Barbeque Sauce

1/2 cup cider vinegar
1/4 cup chili sauce
2 tablespoons lemon juice
1/2 cup light brown sugar
1/4 cup Worcestershire sauce
1 clove garlic, crushed
1/2 cup catsup
1/2 teaspoon dry mustard

Instructions:
In medium saucepan; combine all ingredients for sauce. Simmer, uncovered for 1 hour; stirring occasionally.

Serves 4.

Boston Baked Beans

2 cups navy beans
5 cups water
2 medium onions, chopped
1/2 pound salt pork
1 teaspoon salt
2 teaspoons dry mustard
1/4 cup molasses
1 teaspoon black pepper

Instructions:
Wash beans. Cover with cold water and leave to soak overnight. Drain; reserving 1 1/4 cup of water. Fill dish with beans, onions, and pork. Combine reserved water with remaining ingredients; pour into dish; cover. Cook in a 275 degrees oven for 6 hours; stirring occasionally. Add a little more water if the beans seem slightly dry while cooking.

Serves 4.

Burnt Sugar Syrup Topping

1 1/2 cups sugar
1/2 cup water
1/4 cup butter
1 cup whole blanched almonds

Instructions:
Melt sugar in heavy skillet over low heat. Continue cooking until syrup is deep amber; add water and cook until syrup is smooth. Remove from heat; add butter and stir until melted. Cool.

Serves 4.

Cabbage

1 medium cabbage
2 slices salt pork
1 teaspoon salt
1 teaspoon pepper

Instructions:

Wash cabbage and slice like a watermelon. Place salt pork in large pot and fry. Add cabbage to pot with salt pork and grease from the pork. Add salt and pepper. Cover and cook for 30 minutes.

Serves 4.

Chinese Stir-fry Chicken

3 pounds chicken thighs, boned & cubed
5 tablespoons cornstarch
1/4 teaspoon salt
1 tablespoon sesame oil
1 teaspoon minced fresh ginger
2 tablespoons sherry
1 1/2 tablespoons brown sugar
1/2 lettuce leaves
1/2 cup green onions, chopped
1/4 cup vegetable oil
1/4 teaspoon pepper
2 cloves garlic, minced
1/4 cup water
1 tablespoon cornstarch
1/2 cup parsley, chopped
1/2 cup oyster sauce

Instructions:
Coat chicken with cornstarch. Heat oils and sauté garlic, and ginger until brown. Stir-fry chicken on high heat; sprinkle with salt, pepper and sherry until brown. Reduce to medium heat. Dissolve cornstarch in water, add sugar and oyster sauce; combining well. Pour over chicken; add green onions and parsley. Serve on lettuce leaves.

Serves 4.

Easy Cheesy Sauce

4 slices lite-line cheese
1/2 tablespoon dry mustard
1/4 cup skim milk

Instructions:
In a small sauce pan; combine ingredients over low heat. Cook and stir until lite-line slices melt. Serve over broccoli, Brussels sprouts, baked potato or fish.

Serves 4.

Hog Head Cheese

1 large hog head
4 pigs feet
4 pigs ears
1 cup cider vinegar
4 red peppers
1 teaspoon salt
1/2 teaspoon sage
1 package crackers

Instructions:
Split hog head. Clean thoroughly, removing eyes and brains. Scald. Scrape clean. Place hog head, feet and ears in large stockpot. Simmer about 4 hours or until tender. Remove meat from bone. Place meat in large bowl. Mash. Drain off any fat. Add vinegar, peppers, salt and sage. Stir to combine. Transfer to bowl or dish. Refrigerate 24 hours. Slice. Serve with crackers. 18 servings.

Serves 4.

Homemade Mashed Potatoes

6 potatoes
1/2 cup milk
1 teaspoon black pepper
1 stick butter
1 tablespoon salt
6 cups water

Instructions:

In a large pot, place water and potatoes. Boil until well done. Drain and let stand until cool. Peel potatoes and place in large bowl. Add milk, butter, salt and pepper. Mash until smooth and creamy.

Serves 4.

Mississippi Fried Corn

1 can whole kernel corn
1 tablespoon sugar
1 teaspoon black pepper
1/2 stick butter
1 can cream style corn
1 teaspoon salt
1 teaspoon accent

Instructions:
In frying pan melt butter. Add corn; but drain whole kernel. Add all other ingredients. Cook over low heat 30 minutes; stirring frequently.

Serves 4.

Oyster Stuffing

3 pounds ground pork sausage
1/2 cup green peppers, chopped
1 tablespoon garlic salt
4 cans smoked oysters
1/2 cup onions, chopped
3 tablespoons poultry seasoning
6 egg(s)
1/2 cup celery, chopped
1 tablespoon ground sage

Instructions:
Sauté onion, green pepper, garlic salt, and celery until tender; set aside. Then in pan cook sausage; then add cornbread (see cornbread recipe) and sauté items. Add eggs and all other ingredients; Mix well using your hands.

Serves 4.

Pineapple Sauce

3/4 cup cider vinegar
1 can pineapples, sliced
1 tablespoon soy sauce
1 large green pepper cut crosswise in 1/4 inch circles.
1 cup sugar
1/4 teaspoon ginger
2 tablespoons cornstarch
1 chicken bouillon cubes

Instructions:
Drain pineapple; pouring syrup into 2 cup measure pan add water to make up difference. In medium saucepan combine sugar, cornstarch, pineapple syrup, soy sauce, ginger, bouillon cube, and 3/4 cup cider vinegar. Bring to boil; stirring constantly.

Serves 4.

Spanish Rice

1 cup rice
1 tablespoon cooking oil
1 small bell pepper, chopped
1 small tomato soup, canned
1 small onions, chopped
2 whole tomatoes, diced

Instructions:
In medium pot add oil and rice; stir until brown. Add tomato sauce and one can of water the size of the tomatoes sauce can. Add vegetables and stem until done. Serve hot.

Serves 4.

Zucchini Bread

- 3 egg(s)
- 2 cups sugar
- 2 cups grated raw zucchini
- 2 cups vegetable oil
- 3 teaspoons vanilla
- 3 cups flour
- 1 teaspoon salt
- 1 teaspoon baking powder
- 3 teaspoons cinnamon
- 1 cup chopped walnuts

Instructions:
Preheat oven to 350 degrees. Butter 2 one pound loaf pans. Beat eggs until light and foamy. Add sugar, oil, zucchini and vanilla. Do not over mix. Combine dry ingredients and stir into zucchini mixture. Add nuts and pour into pans. Bake for 60 minutes. Cool on wire rack.

Serves 4.

Zucchini with Fresh Herbs

2 pounds zucchini
1 teaspoon salt
1 teaspoon black pepper
1/4 cup butter, melted
2 tablespoons chopped parsley
1 tablespoon snipped chives or dill
1 tablespoon lemon juice

Instructions:
Wash zucchini; cut into diagonal, 1/4 inch thick slices. In medium skillet with tight-fitting cover, bring 1/3 cup water with salt and pepper boiling. Add zucchini; cook over medium heat, covered, 10 minutes, or until just tender, but not mushy (water should be evaporated). Add butter, parsley, chives, and lemon juice; toss gently to combine. Turn into heated serving dish.

SUPPER

Cornbread

3 cups yellow cornmeal
1 teaspoon salt
1 1/2 cups milk
1 1/2 cups flour
3 egg(s)
1 cup water
2 tablespoons baking powder
1/2 cup Wesson oil

Instructions:
Mix all ingredients together and bake at 350 degrees for about 1/2 hour.

Serves 4.

Da'thy's 7-Bone Roast

6 pounds bone roast
2 teaspoons butter
1 clove garlic
1 teaspoon black pepper
6 white potatoes, halved
2 tablespoons seasoning salt
2 teaspoons salad oil
1 small onion(s)
1 teaspoon salt
1 teaspoon accent
2 cups water
3 tablespoons flour

Instructions:
Wipe roast with paper towel. Preheat oven to 350 degrees. Cut two holes in each side of the roast and place garlic inside holes. In a large skillet, pour oil and butter over medium heat. Sprinkle on both sides of roast, accent, salt, pepper, and seasoned salt; then rub thoroughly over both sides of the roast the flour. Then place the roast in hot oil and butter. Brown on both sides until golden brown. Take out of skillet and place into roasting pan. Add two cups of water. Slice onion over the roast; cover and place in oven for 1 hour. Take the roast out of oven; turn over and add potatoes; return to oven and cook another hour; but reduce heat to 300 degrees. Add more water if desired.

Serves 4.

Da'thy's Meat Sauce

1 pound ground beef
1 teaspoon sweet basil
1 teaspoon black pepper
1 teaspoon seasoning salt
1/2 cup celery, chopped
1/2 cup onion, chopped
1 can tomato paste
4 cups water
1 teaspoon oregano
1 teaspoon accent
1 teaspoon garlic salt
1 teaspoon salt
1/2 cup bell pepper, chopped
2 bay leaves
1 can small can whole peeled tomatoes
1/2 cup sugar

Instructions:
In large saucepan brown ground beef. Add all other ingredients except sugar. Stir well. Reduce heat to simmer for 3 hours; stirring occasionally. Add sugar and cook 30 minutes more. Serve over paghetti.

SALAD

Food Potato Salad

6 medium potatoes
6 egg(s)
1/2 mayonnaise
1 medium onions, chopped
1 teaspoon salt
6 cups water
1/2 cup sugar teaspoon black pepper teaspoon accent

Instructions:

In large pot place potatoes and water boil until well done about 2 hours. Take potatoes out of water and let cool. Peel potatoes and cut-up. Boil eggs and cut-up. Add both together. Mix mayo, onion, salt pepper and accent and add to potato mixture. Add sugar mix well. Transfer to bowl and place in refrigerator for 1 hour.

AFTERWORD

LESAH~
Mom's cooking creates the most memorable moments! Whenever I think of any joyous occasion with family, her cooking was always at the very center of it! Her dishes are made with so much pride and love.., the memory of how delicious her beautiful array of delightful dishes are, will last us all a lifetime! Food that surely nourishes the soul- true soul food! Among my many favorites is her turkey and dressing! Slowly cooked to perfection, juicy with every bite! And the dressing, well, let's just call that dreamy!!! Full of seasonings and wholesome goodness! I am so grateful for this wonderful culinary heritage! The lasting legacy being every taste filled with her love for all of the family!

ELIYAH~
I love my grandma's Mac n' Cheese! I think it is the best in the world! I always think of grandma's cooking and happy times! Happy times and grandma's cooking go hand in hand! When all of the family comes together, my cousins and I always talk about what food or dessert we like most!!! We always laugh because we always hope that she made plenty of our favorites to go back for seconds... and thirds!!! I love my grandma because she puts her love and soul into her cooking! I hope to be able to create special moments like that for my family when I am older! Thanks grandma, you're the best cook in the world to me!

ELISHUJAH~
It was love at first... "BITE"!! LOL I am talking about the first time, and every single time after that, I tasted my granny's potato salad! Who knew a potato could taste so good!! I am convinced that it has

to be God and my granny's touch that could make a potato taste that good!!! When mom says grandma is cooking for the holidays, that to me goes along with the true meaning of Thanksgiving, or any other holiday for that matter- a time to thank God for all of His goodness, to thank God for my beautiful family and all He has done for us, and thank Him for my granny's potato salad! I have some of the fondest memories of my life with her potato salad!! Me and my cousins try to see who can eat the most!! It is so good and it makes me feel her love for us! I vote my granny's cooking as the best in the world! And I think everyone in world should have a taste of her love, LOL, I mean her cooking, especially her potato salad! I love you grandma! Thanks for introducing me to the first love! LOL!

INDEX

A
Apple Pie, 48

B
Baked Fish, 12
Banana Nut Bread, 49
Barbecue Spareribs, 13
Barbeque Sauce, 90
Beef Liver and Onions, 6
Big Leroy's Skillet Beef & Macaroni, 14
Boiled Pig Feet, 15
Boston Baked Beans, 91
Braised Duck with Beer, 16
Breaded Veal Cutlet, 17
Burnt Sugar Syrup Topping, 92
Buttered Beans with Chopped Ham, 18
Buttermilk Hush Puppies, 70

C
Cabbage, 93
Chicken Casserole, 71
Chicken Gizzards with Rice, 72
Chicken Tetrazzini, 19
Chicken with Biscuit Crisps, 73
Chili Tacos, 75
Chili, 74
Chinese Stir-fry Chicken, 94
Chocolate Pound Cake, 50
Clam Fritters, 2

Collard Greens and Ham Hocks or Smoked Turkey Tail, 20
Collard Greens with Neck bones, 21
Corn Oysters, 22
Cornbread, 106
Cornish Hen with Wild Rice, 23
Cottage Cheese Jell-O Salad, 51
Cumberland Sauce. 24

D
Da'thy's Lobster Newburg, 25
Da'thy's 7-Bone Roast, 107
Da'thy's Baked Turkey with Oyster Stuffing, 26
Da'thy's Meat Sauce, 108
Da'thy's Pineapple Chicken, 76
Da'thy's Quick Chicken and Dumplings, 77
Da'thy's Can't Get Enough Peach Cobbler, 52
Da'thy's Can't Stop Eat'em Candie Yams, 53
Da'thy's Mississippi Curry Chicken, 27
Da'thy's Mississippi Fried Chicken, 78
Da'thy's Mississippi Pound Cake, 54
Da'thy's Mouth Watering Sweet Potato Pie, 55
Da'thy's Sock-It-To-Me Baked Macaroni and Cheese, 79
Da'thy's Fast Chili, 80
Da'thy's Quick Meatloaf, 81

E
Easy Cheesy Sauce, 95
Easy To Make Meat Loaf, 28

F
Fairy Mississippi Rolls, 7
Fried Cat Fish Nuggets, 82
Fried Chicken Gizzards, 83
Fried Fish, 84
Fried Potatoes, 8

G
German Sweet Chocolate Cake, 56
Ginger Cookies, 57
Gumbo, 29

H
Hoe Cakes, 58
Hog Head Cheese, 96
Homemade Mashed Potatoes, 97
Honey Baked Ham, 30

J
Jamiya's Fast N Easy Biscuits, 9
Jell-O Lemon Pudding Cake, 59
Jessie Palmer's Bake Burgers, 85

K
Kentucky Bourbon Sweet Potatoes, 60

L
Lemon Chicken, 31
Lime Pie, 61

M
Meatballs N Gravy, 32
Mississippi Banana Pudding, 62
Mississippi Fried Corn, 98
Mississippi Fried Steak and Gravy, 33
Mississippi Hearty Beef Stew, 34
Mississippi Pecan Pie, 63
Mississippi Smothered Rabbit with gravy, 35
Mississippi Smothered Steak, 36
Mixed Greens, 37
Molasses Brown Bread, 64

O
Oven Fried Chicken, 38
Oyster Stuffing, 99

P
Peanut Butter Bon Bars, 65
Pie Crust, 66
Pineapple Duck. 39
Pineapple Sauce, 100
Pinto Beans and Ham Hocks, 40
Pork Chitterlings, 41
Pork Neck Bones and Black Eye Peas, 42
Potato Salad, 110

Pumpkin Pie, 67

R
Roast Hen with Stuffing, 43

S
Sausage Rice Casserole, 86
Sautéed Bananas, 68
Scrambled Eggs with Ham, 10
Spanish Rice, 101
Summer Squash Casserole, 87
Sweet and Sour Chicken Wings, 3
Sweet and Sour Meatballs, 44

T
Turkey Parts with Rice, 45

V
Veal with Sauce, 46

Z
Zucchini Bread, 102
Zucchini with Fresh Herbs, 103

ORDER FORM

Telephone: 909-301-1993
Email: ptpoutreach@aol.com
Orders accepted by check addressed to:
D. Woods, 832 W 21ST Street. San Bernardino, CA, 92405
Name: _____
Address: _____
City: _____
State: _____
Zip: _____
Telephone: _____
Email: _____
Qty: _____

Shipping is via US Mail: $14.99/book, plus $4.00 shipping and handling.

Made in the USA
Monee, IL
26 August 2020

www.ingramcontent.com/pod-product-compliance
Lightning Source LLC
LaVergne TN
LVHW091558060526
838200LV00036B/889